Perry Armstrong

The Piasa

The Devil among the Indians

Perry Armstrong

The Piasa
The Devil among the Indians

ISBN/EAN: 9783337303877

Printed in Europe, USA, Canada, Australia, Japan

Cover: Foto ©ninafisch / pixelio.de

More available books at **www.hansebooks.com**

THE PIASA,

OR,

THE DEVIL AMONG THE INDIANS.

BY

HON. P. A. ARMSTRONG,

AUTHOR OF "THE SAUKS, AND THE BLACK HAWK WAR,"
"LEGEND OF STARVED ROCK," ETC.

WITH ENGRAVINGS OF THE MONSTERS.

MORRIS, ILL.:
E. B. FLETCHER, BOOK AND JOB PRINTER.
1887.

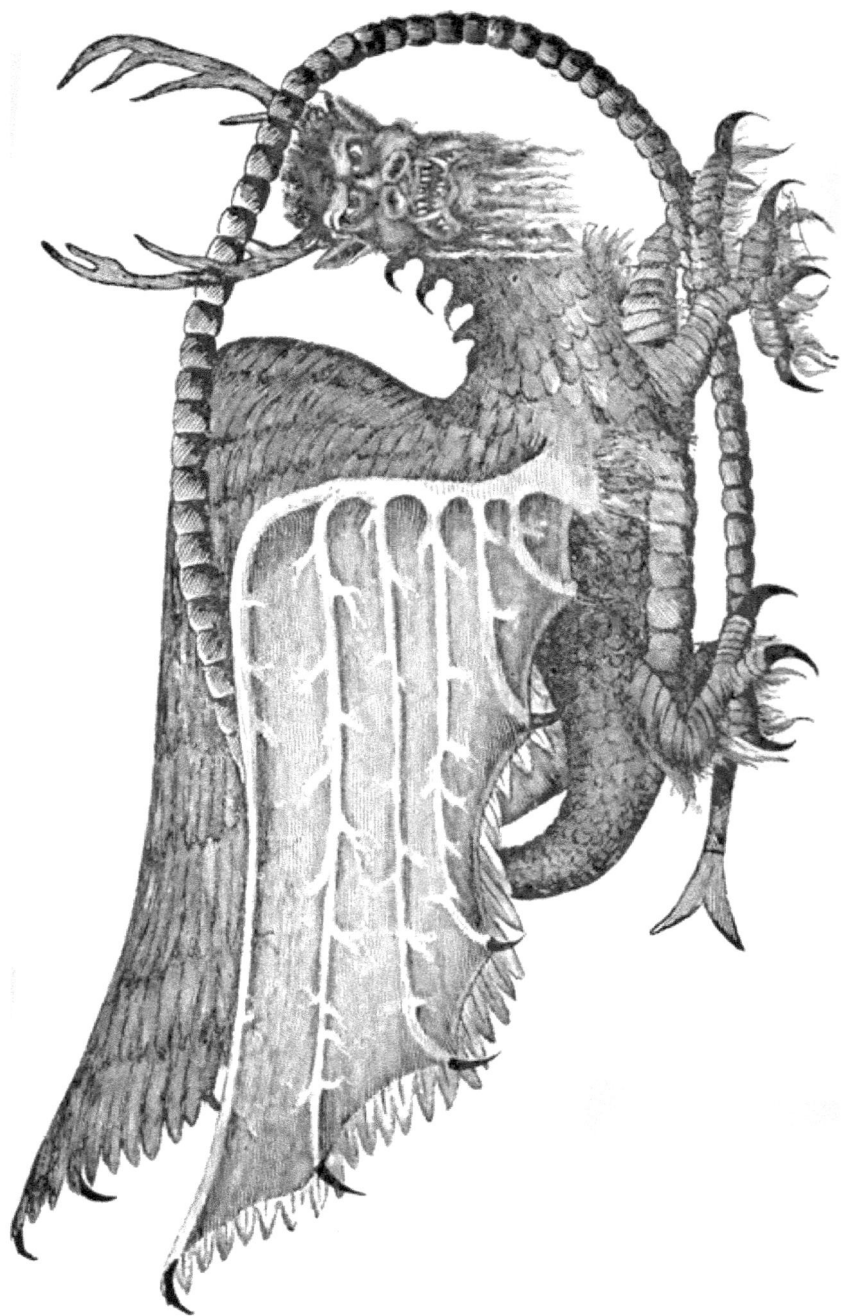

CHAPTER I.

PICTOGRAPHS AND PETROGLYPHS—THEIR ORIGIN AND USES—THE PIASA,* OR PIUSA,† THE LARGEST AND MOST WONDERFUL PETROGLYPHS OF THE WORLD—THEIR CLOSE RESEMBLANCE TO THE MANIFOLD DESCRIPTIONS AND NAMES OF THE DEVIL OF THE SCRIPTURES — WHERE, WHEN AND BY WHOM THESE MONSTER PETROGLYPHS WERE DISCOVERED—BUT BY WHOM CONCEIVED AND EXECUTED, AND FOR WHAT PURPOSE, NOW IS, AND PROBABLY EVER WILL BE, A SEALED MYSTERY.

From the evening and the morning of the sixth day, from the beginning when God created the heaven and the earth, and darkness was upon the face of the deep, and the spirit of God moved upon the face of the waters, and God said: Let there be light in the firmament of the heavens to divide the day from the night, and give light upon the earth, and made two great lights, the greater to rule the day and the lesser to rule the night, and plucked from his jeweled crown a handful of diamonds and scattered them broadcast athwart the sky for brilliants to his canopy, and stars in his firmament, down through the countless ages to the present, all nations, tongues, kindreds and peoples, in whatsoever condition, time, clime or place, civilized, pagan, Mohammedan, barbarian or savage, have adopted and utilized signs, motions, gestures, types, emblems, symbols, pictures, drawings, etchings or paintings as their primary and most natural as well as direct and forcible methods and vehicles of communicating, recording and perpetuating thought and history. Even that great book of books and history of histories—the Holy Bible—teems with examples of this character

---

*PY-A-SAW—That is, the beast that devours men.

†PY-U-SAW—That is, the bird that devours men.

from the first chapter of Genesis to the last chapter of Revelations. Our syllabaries or alphabets are but a series and system of types, symbols and emblems which, by the aid of machinery and printers' ink, bristle with thought and are the vehicles of recording history.

Sign or gesture language is the primary method of direct communication, from the beginning to the present, while object language is, and ever has been, the indirect mode of not only communicating but preserving history. The former is of more universal use than the latter, for it always has and always will exist and be utilized by the entire human family, civilized or savage, and extends to every animal existence, flesh, fish and fowl.

While gesture language is direct, it is but transient, because not recorded so as to be preserved. On the other hand object language is direct in its communication and most graphically and indelibly recorded.

The entire series of object language may well be embraced in the term now in general use—pictograph—or a writing by pictures, which conveys upon sight and instantaneously records by graphic means the thought, act or deed intended by the artist, without words, syllables or letters, and may be delineated upon any hard substance—wood, stone, metal, bone, slate, dried hide, etc.

When delineated upon rock or stone these pictographs have been aptly named petroglyphs by the learned German archæologist, Dr. Andree, of Stuttgardt, which means rock delineations, or pictures.

By signs or gestures the infant first attempts and finally succeeds in attracting attention and indicating its wants, and no other means of communication is known between persons entirely ignorant of each other's language and deaf mutes. The secondary method is by sounds or oral language, which is of the greatest importance and universal use.

Object language, or pictographs, is the tertiary method, and though not so generally used, its communication being of a more permanent and enduring form, its lessons are of greater importance in history than sign or oral language. There can be no doubt of the fact that pictographs were the precursors and parents of our syllabaries or alphabets, and the indirect expressions of ideas formed in oral speech, hence their importance to the ethnologist depends upon the light they may shed upon the evolution of human culture. If by their aid we may learn the wisdom of the ages in which no written history was kept except these crude pictures, then indeed will they have served a noble purpose.

The importance of pictographs to the human race cannot be over-estimated in their production of the smaller and systematized letters and types which have been the direct means of preserving and perpetuating history, science and knowledge, through the alphabet which seems to have been known and brought into use some 3,400 years ago or about 1,500 years before the Christian era. Whether letters and the alphabet were invented by the Egyptians, Ninevehans, Phœnicians or Chinese is a disputed question, for they all claim the honor. Rollin says letters were taken from Syria to Greece by Cadmus about the year 1455 B. C.

The first discovery of pictographs and petroglyphs in the United States dates back only about three hundred years, but they are more plentiful in this than any other country; and the American Indians have shown a versatility as well as much talent in their execution, as well as design. Indeed they have in many instances combined the art of etching, or engraving, and that of painting with fine effect, and seem to have had some practical aim or object in view in the production of each delineation. To be enabled to correctly interpret and fairly understand the purport and meaning of Indian pictographs, and more especially their petroglyphs, which are of greater interest and importance to the ethnologist and archæologist, we must become familiar with their traditions, mythologies, customs, habits, dress, religious beliefs and modes of worship. Their petroglyphs as a rule being much larger than their pictographs, and incised or cut into the face of the rock and the incisions or tracings filled with paint, they are much better preserved as well as larger than their pictographs. Add to this the fact that the Indian is naturally averse to manual labor, and the cutting or engraving of the hard rock with such instruments as he could improvise was slow and tedious work, none but the most important objects and events were delineated upon the rocks, hence their petroglyphs are vastly more important as records than their pictographs. Again, there is another difference between these two kinds of delineations, viz: All their pictographs we can or have found are of comparatively modern date, while their petroglyphs as a rule are ancient. This may be accounted for, in part at least, by the fact that their pictographs were simply painted and usually on perishable material, while their petroglyphs were etched, cut or incised and then painted, and the painting renewed from time to time, kept them well preserved. A very general system of pictographs is now in use by the Indians of the plains, by means of which they keep a record of the leading events of each year which thereby becomes an annual calendar, which they call winter counts. Not infrequently do they keep this kind of chronology for a century upon a single buffalo hide. That of Lone Dog, a Dakota Indian, embraces over seventy years and covers only about half the surface of one buffalo robe. These pictographs commenced with the year 1800, near the center of the robe, and subsequent years up to 1872 are arranged in elliptical circles around it. The first year is represented by three sets of parallel black lines of ten each, showing that thirty Dakotas were killed by the Crow Indians that year. The next year is represented by the naked bust of an Indian, literally covered with red blotches, showing that small-pox killed many Indians that year, etc. Many of these pictographs are apt illustrations of the ideologies intended to be conveyed. The meteoric shower of November 13, 1833, is represented by a picture of the moon and a host of falling stars, leaving a large streak trailing after each. Indian pictographs may be numbered by hundreds of thousands in the United States while their petroglyphs are comparatively few, less than one to a thousand, yet they have been found all over the country from Maine to California, on rocks, boulders, ledges, canyons, caves and grottoes. Sandstone surface especially is prolific with these delineations, and are of three classes.

1st. Simply paintings upon the rocks, usually in three colors, red, green and black.

2nd. Etched or cut upon the rock.

3rd. First incised, or etched, and then painted, the lines of paint following the incised lines. The first above described kind is far more numerous than either of the others.

The Indians not only understand the art of compounding and mixing paints that withstand the elements, but are adepts in that art. Though they know nothing of the use of linseed oil and turpentine in the preparation of paint they have a substitute which is more lasting. By boiling the tails of the beaver together with the feet of the elk, deer, moose or antelope, they obtain a glutinous, oily substance with which they mix their earth-pigments and oxides of iron, copper and zinc, burnt bone, etc., whereby they are able to produce colors of the most enduring kind. Though the Indian never understood the art of blending colors so as to produce varieties of shade, he well understood primary colors and used them to advantage in producing all the prismatic shades. Their paint brushes were constructed of small pieces of soft wood, chewed or pounded at the end into fibers, but more recently they used tufts of antelope hair tied around small sticks. Their implements for drawing, etching, cutting, carving, scratching, pecking or engraving petroglyphs were few and decidedly pristine and simple. They consisted of small pieces of sharp-pointed rocks—obsidian, flint and quartz predominating. But after coming in contact with white people the Indians soon discovered the great superi-

ority of well-tempered steel over the very best qualities of obsidian or quartz in the manufacture of gravers for stone etchings,
and have very generally adopted a short thick-bladed knife for
that purpose. For tracing pens they used a piece of dry buffalo
rib or hard wood, dipped in a thin, colored glue which was
spread along the line intended to delineate the object of the
petroglyph. The tracings served as lines for incising, scratching
and pecking, as well as for final painting. Like every other
nation and people of earth the red man attaches great signifi-
cance to colors. To them black is an emblem of sorrow, anguish
and death; red of defiance, anger and war; yellow of treachery,
jealousy and inconstancy; green of hope, joy and victory; blue
of truth, love and constancy. By arranging the cardinal colors
side by side in various forms they had a species of sign alphabet
by means whereof they communicated as well as perpetuated a
large amount of information and history. Nearly every rock-
cavern, as well as smooth-faced perpendicular ledge of any considerable altitude throughout the entire western hemisphere,
when discovered by the white man, were converted into maps,
charts and histories by the aborigines, whereon were recorded
in that most graphic language, petroglyphs, the great events
of the preceding ages, and could we but correctly read and fully
interpret this silent language, the early history of the occident,
like that of the orient, would teem with deeds of heroism and
daring. The rocks at Oakley Springs, Arizona, and the valley
of the Kanawha, West Virginia, alone would furnish an ency-
clopedia of stirring events of the most intense interest. The
valley of the Mississippi, though producing but comparatively
few petroglyphs, exhibited some of the grandest and by far the
most mysterious ever found in this or any other country in the
world, known as the Piasa, and described by Father Marquette,
the celebrated Jesuit priest, who was of noble descent and born
in Picardy, France, and came as a missionary to Canada in the
year 1665, where he soon learned to speak the language of some
half dozen Indian tribes, from whom he heard of the existence

of a great river in the west which they called Mesche-eebe, or
the great river. Some of them called it Nanne-sipon, or the
river of fishes; others called it Chusa-gua, Sassa-gonly, and
Mala-bianchi, and subsequently the French caled it La Palisade
Escandido, Colbert, or St. Louis. M. Talon was the French
intendant of Canada at the time, but had been ordered to Paris
in the fall of 1672. From Marquette and others he had heard
stories about this great unknown river of the west and determined to investigate the matter. Before leaving Canada he
selected M. Joliet a successful merchant of Quebec, who had
much experience among the Indians, to conduct the expedition.
Joliet selected Marquette as his chief assistant and adviser to
accompany him in this hazardous enterprise, and on the 13th of
May, 1673, with only about a half dozen men they embarked in
their canoes and struck out on their long, lonesome and danger-
ous voyage of discovery. They did not reach the Mississippi until
the 17th of June. Marquette says (See his discoveries of the Mississippi, published in Paris in 1681): "We here met from time to
time numberless fish which struck so violently against our canoes
that at first we took them to be large trees which threatened
to upset us. * * * As we were descending the river we saw
high rocks with hideous monsters painted on them and upon
which the bravest Indian dare not look. They are as large as
a calf, with head and horns like a goat, their eyes are red, beard
like a tiger's and a face like a man's. Their tails are so long
that they pass over their bodies and between their legs under
their bodies, ending like a fish's tail. They are painted red, green
and black, and so well drawn that I could not believe they were
drawn by the Indians, and for what purpose they were drawn
seems to me a mystery." Again he says: "Passing the mouth
of the Illinois we soon fell into the shadow of a tall promontory,
and with great astonishment beheld the representation of two
monsters painted on its lofty limestone front. Each of these
frightful figures had the face of a man, the horns of a deer, the
beard of a tiger, and the tail of a fish, so long that it passed

around the body, over the head and between the legs.   It was
an object of Indian worship, and greatly impressed me with the
necessity of substituting for this monstrous idolatry the true
God."

Father Hennepin, another early explorer of the wilds of the
west, published a small volume in 1698 entitled, "A new discovery of a vast Country in America," which he dedicated to
William III, King of Great Britain, says, pages 168 to 170:
"This made our voyage the more easie, for our men landed
several times to kill some Fowl and other Game with which the
Banks of the Mischasipi are plentifully stocked; however, before
we came to the River Illinois we discovered Messorites who
came down along the River, but as they had no Pyrogues with
them we crossed to the other side, and to avoid any surprise
during the night we made no fire and thereby the Savages could
not discover whereabouts we were, for doubtless they would
have murthered us, thinking we were their enemies.

"I had quite forgot to relate that the Illinois had told us
that towards the Cape which I have called in my map St.
Anthony, near the nation of the Messorites, there were some
Tritons and other Sea Monsters painted which the boldest Men
durst not look upon, there being some Inchantment in their
face.   I thought this was a story, but when we came near the
place they had mentioned we saw instead of these Monsters a
Horse and some other Beasts painted upon the Rock with Red
Colors by the Savages.   The Illinois had told us likewise that
the rock on which these dreadful Monsters stood was so steep
that no man could climb up to it, but had we not been afraid
of the Savages more than of the Monsters we had certainly got
up to them.   There is a common Tradition amongst the people
that a great number of Miamis were drowned in that place,
being pursued by the Savages of Matsegamie, and since that
time the Savages going by the Rock use to smoak and offer
Tobacco to these Beasts to appease, as they say, the Manitou,
that is, in the Language of the Algonquins and Accadians, an

Evil Spirit, which the Iroquois call Otkon, but the Name is the only thing they know of him. While I was at Quebec I understood M. Jolliet had been upon the Mischasipi and obliged to return without going down the River because of the Monsters I have spoken of who had frighted him, as also because he was afraid to be taken by the Spaniards, and having an opportunity to know the truth of that Storey from M. Jolliet himself, with whom I had often traveled upon the River St. Lawrence, I asked him whether he had been as far as the Arkansas. That Gentleman answered me that the Outtaouats had often spoke to him of these Monsters, but that he had never gone further than the Hurons and Outtaouats, with whom he had remained to exchange our companie's Commodities with their Furs. He added that the Savages had told him that it was not safe to go down the River because of the Spaniards. But notwithstanding this Report I have found nowhere upon the River any mark as crosses and the like that could persuade me that the Spaniards had been there and the Savages inhabiting the Mischasipi would not have expressed such admiration as they did when they saw us if they had seen Europeans before. I'll examine the question more in my second volume."

In his second volume Hennepin says he had seen Father Marquette, from whom he got the following description: "Along the Rocks I have mentioned we have found one very high and steep and saw two Monsters painted upon it which are so hideous that we were frighted at the first sight, and the boldest Savage dare not for their Eyes look upon them. They are drawn as big as a Calf, with two horns like a Wild Goat. Their Eyes are Red, their Beard is like that of a Tyger, and their Body is covered with Scales. Their Tail is so long that it goes over their Heads and then turns between their Fore-Legs under the Belly, ending like a Fish-Tail. There are but three Colors, viz: Red, Green and Black, but those Monsters are so well drawn that I cannot believe that the Savages did it, and the Rock whereon they are painted is so steep that it is a wonder to me how it was possible to draw those Figures. But to know to what purpose they were made is a great Mystery. Whatever it be our best Painters would hardly do better."

Two immensely large petroglyphs of a monster—or more properly speaking, monsters, for they do not appear to have been alike, though substantially so, as will be seen by reference to the engravings herewith given—were found, first incised or cut upon a layer of bluish gray sandstone overlying a bed of limestone on the north bank of the Mississippi, immediately where the Illinois State prison was built at Alton, Illinois, which were quite distinct when that locality was first settled by the white people, and traces of their outlines remained until the rock whereon they were delineated was quarried by the convicts of the penitentiary as late as about the year 1856. From the mouth of the Illinois river at Grafton to Alton, Illinois, a distance of twenty miles, the Mississippi river runs from west to east, and its north bank or Illinois side is a high bluff, the highest point being the eastern end. This bluff is but a continuous perpendicular strata of limestone, ranging from forty to fifty feet high, with a layer of bluish gray fine grit sandstone, about twenty feet deep, lying on the top or over the limestone, and upon this sandstone, at an elevation of some eighty feet above the base of this ledge of rocks and the river's surface, these monsters were incised and afterwards painted. They were of about equal size and measured thirty feet in length by twelve feet in height. From their hideous shape and size they were a mortal terror to all the Indian nations of the then northwest. Each nation had one or more traditions connected therewith, some calling them *The Piasa*, others called them *The Piusa*. In painting these monsters but three colors were used—red, emblematic of war and vengeance; black, symbolic of death and despair; and green, expressive of hope and triumph over death in the land of dreams, beneath, beyond the evening star, where they located their happy hunting grounds.

In estimating the size of these petroglyphs, Father Marquette did not take into consideration their great elevation nor the distance from his canoe to the rock wall where they were delineated. Why he did not mention the fact of their having the wings of a bat, but of the shape of an eagle's, is not easily explained, yet as a matter of fact they were both supplied with those appendages beyond a doubt, as there are several persons still living who bear testimony to the fact from having seen them. They also had four legs, each supplied with eagle-shaped talons. The combination and blending together of the master species of the earth, sea and air, as shown in these petroglyphs so as to present the leading and most terrific characteristics of the various species thus graphically arranged, is an absolute wonder and seems to show a vastly superior knowledge of animal, fowl, reptile and fish nature than has been accorded to the Indian. Indeed, they seem to have been made by some person familiar with the Holy Scriptures, for we read from them as follows: "And the first beast was like a lion and the second like a calf, and the third beast had a face as a man, and the fourth beast was like a flying eagle. * * * As for the likeness of their faces they four had the face of a man and the face of a lion on the right side, and the face of an ox on the left side; they four also had the head of an eagle. * * * And their wings were stretched upwards, and when they went I heard the noise of their wings like the noise of great waters. * * * The first was like a lion, and had eagle's wings. * * * And another beast, like a leopard, appeared, which had upon its back four wings of a fowl. * * * And a fourth beast appeared, dreadful and terrible, and exceedingly strong, and it had great iron teeth. * * * And behold, a great red dragon, having seven heads and ten horns, and his tail drew the third part of the stars. * * * And he had two horns like a lamb, and he spake like a dragon. * * * And to the woman were given two wings of an eagle, that she might fly into the wilderness. Behold, there came up from the sea an eagle. * * * And she spread her wings over all the earth, and all the winds of the air blew on her and were gathered together. * * * And I beheld as it were a roaring lion chased out of the woods, and I saw he sent a man's voice unto the eagle. * * * And therefore appear no more, thou eagle nor thy horrible wings, nor thy wicked feathers, nor thy malicious heads, nor thy hurtful claws, nor all thy vain body."

These quotations from the Holy Scriptures might be extended to a great length, all tending to show that the ancient Israelites believed in the existence of a veritable corporeal and visible Devil, to whom they attributed the power of all evil, and symbolized under various forms, shapes and names. To Mother Eve he assumed the shape of the serpent, with the voice of a man, and by false representations and blandishments induced her to dupe and deceive her husband. While more generally described in the Bible as the leviathan or dragon, he is frequently mentioned as the "old serpent," "enemy," "evil spirit," "unclean spirit," "evil one," "wicked one," "liar," "lying spirit," "father of lies," "crooked serpent," "piercing serpent," "prince of the power of the air," "great red dragon," "abaddon," "beast," "apollyon," "adversary," "accuser of his brethren," "serpent," "spirit that worketh in the children of disobedience," "Belial," "Beelzebub," "god of this world," "power of darkness," "ruler of the darkness of this world," "prince of the devils," "tempter," "murderer," "devil," "Satan," etc.

All of these names and terms were used as being synonymous and convertible, representing a fixed, firm and abiding faith in the existence of one or more all-bad being, essence or principle, which is the active and implacable enemy of the human race. Though indefinite and divergent in opinion as to whether there were but one or a legion of these evil spirits, agencies or devils, as well as to whether they had a real definite corporeal or merely a spiritual existence, it is a significant fact that all nations, kindreds and tongues in every clime, time and place, whether Christian, Mohammedan or savage, are united in one great prevailing faith and belief in the existence of certain agencies or spirits which are ever busy in making mischief among, and causing sorrow, pain, grief and suffering to the people of earth, to which they apply as many different names, shapes and attributes as the stars in heaven. Nor do they confine the persecutions of these evil spirits to their earthly existence, but connect them with vivid imagination to that other and fondly-hoped-for better life beyond the grave, whither they fear these tormentors will follow them.

In very many leading characteristics, customs and beliefs the North American Indians very closely resemble those of the ancient Israelites, when they first came in contact with the Europeans. Like them they believed in the existence of one great and all-powerful being or spirit which should be and was the object of adoration. Of the God-head or Christ they had no tradition, and consequently no belief; hence the subtleties and nice distinctions of the trinity, Father, Son and Holy Ghost of the Christian they did not comprehend and would not believe. Red Jacket said: "If the Great Spirit so loved the pale-faces that he sent his only son to them, and they killed him, then the white people did very wrong, and should be punished for this evil deed. If he had sent his son to the red men he would have been well fed and kindly treated."

Though the Indians, like Christianized white men, believe in the existence of a multiplicity of good spirits, one alone is chief, whom they know as the Manitou or Sowana, corresponding with our God or Jehovah, and the universality of this belief in the existence of an all-powerful Supreme Ruler of the universe among all nations and peoples of earth constitutes the strongest argument and most irrefragable proof of the existence and active agency of an indulgent, loving Father or God, whose heart-yearnings are constantly leading and drawing his children home.

"Where buds and flowers of blooming spring
    In brightest robes abound,
And sweetest odors constant bring
    In never ceasing round ,
Where birds of richest plumage shine,
    Of fairy form and fair,
And softest melodies combine
    To charm the vocal air."

The celebrated Sauk chief, Black Hawk, who, all things considered, was probably the ablest Indian that ever lived, and certainly one of the purest and noblest of his race, said: "The Great Spirit has the care of all beings created. * * * Some believe in two spirits, one good, the other bad, and make feasts for the bad spirit, to keep him quiet, thinking that if they can make peace with him the good spirit will not hurt them. * * If the Great and Good Spirit wishes us to believe and do as the whites, he could easily change our opinions, so that we could see, think and act as they do. We are nothing as compared to His power, and we feel and know it. We have men among us like the whites, who pretend to know the right path, but will not consent to show it without pay. I have no faith in their path, but believe every man must make his own path."

Red Jacket said: "If the Great Spirit desires us to believe in the white man's religion why has He not given us a book like the one he gave them, that we might read and understand His will? * * * He knows what is best for His red children, and we do but follow His will." But Black Hawk, with all his piety and sound judgment, believed in manifold good and bad spirits, as illustrated by his idea as to how corn, beans and tobacco were first discovered by his race, which was that "a beautiful woman was seen to descend from the clouds and alight upon the earth by two of our ancestors who had killed a deer and were sitting by the fire roasting a part of it to eat. They were astonished at seeing her, and concluded she was hungry and had smelt the meat. They immediately went to her, taking with them a piece of the roasted venison. They presented it to her. She ate it, telling them to return to the spot where she was sitting at the end of one year and they would find a reward for their kindness and generosity. She then ascended to the clouds and disappeared. The men returned to their village and explained to the tribe what they had seen, done and heard, but were laughed at by their people. When the period had arrived for them to visit this consecrated ground where they were to find a reward for their attention to the beautiful woman of the clouds, they went with a large party, and found where her right hand had rested on the ground corn growing, where the left hand had rested, beans, and immediately where she had been seated, tobacco."

In speaking of the island of Rock Island the old chieftain said: "It was our garden, like the white people have near their big villages, which supplied us with strawberries, blackberries, gooseberries, plums, apples and nuts. * * * A good spirit had charge of it, which lived in a cave in the rock immediately under the place where the fort now stands (old Fort Armstrong, torn down in 1845). This guardian spirit has often been seen by our people. It was white, with large wings like a swan's, but ten times larger. We were particular not to make much noise in that part of the island which it inhabited for fear of disturbing it, but the noise at the fort has since driven it away, and no doubt a bad spirit has taken its place."

He does not claim to have ever seen this good white spirit, with wings ten times larger than those of a swan, which would make it fully as large as the Piasa, but says that many of his people had seen it. Thus it is apparent that the Indians believed in the corporeal existence of winged spirits, both good and bad, and to their minds all that was good and desirable was attributed to good spirits, while all that was terrible and disastrous was charged to the account of bad spirits. By referring to the two engravings given as the Piasa, or Piusa, it will be observed that the artist who originated and executed them has embodied all the more dreadful characteristics contained in the foregoing Biblical descriptions of the devil. Here do we behold the wings and talons of the eagle, united to the body of the dragon or alligator, with the face of a man, the horns of the black-tailed deer or elk, the nostrils of the hippopotamus, the teeth and beard of the tiger, the ears of the fox, and the tail of the serpent, or fish, with the scales of the salamander, so nicely arranged and fitted together as to preserve the distinctive characteristics of each and produce a picture of all that is the most horrible, alike in animal, fowl, fish and reptile nature in a single graphic view. That king of birds, the eagle, has ever been considered by all nations and peoples the emblem and symbol of speed, strength, ferocity and quick perception. The deer and elk, the fleetest of the animal creation, and the tiger the most pugnacious and ferocious. The fox is the symbol of cunning, and possesses the sharpest sense of hearing. The hippopotamus is indigenous alike to land and sea, with the strength and courage of the lion, united to the ferocity of the tiger, and a hide which may be termed bullet-proof. The dragon as above shown is the prototype and representative of Satan, and the serpent is his twin brother, while man is the image of his Maker, and by divine command received "dominion over the fish of the sea, and over the fowl of the air, and over every living thing that moveth upon the earth." Whether conceived and executed by the Indian, Mound Builder or white man, these petroglyphs were fearfully grand in conception and stupendously large in dimension. Some writers in describing them have said their scales rivaled the rainbow in their gaudy colorings, but we are inclined to the opinion they were in error in that respect. The Mississippi was the great highway of travel to the Indians, which forced them against their will to pass these pictured monsters. Knowing this fact the Indian voyagers as a rule prepared for an attack upon these petroglyphs as they passed, while some offered sacrifices and burnt offerings to appease their supposed anger toward the worshippers, others offered prayer and supplications to them for mercy and forgiveness, or set up a doleful howl, accompanied with objurgations and lamentations, but the great mass of the braves and warriors sent poisoned arrow heads and bullets at them, so that between the hail and storms of a long, long period of time, together with the indentations made by arrow heads and bullets the whole face of the rock where these petroglyphs were delineated was pitted as if from a severe attack of small-pox, which fact led to the belief that

the scales were variegated in color. Yet it is possible they were
painted of different colors. If such was the case these petroglyphs must have presented a most beautifully horrid sight,
rendering them far above any other specimen of aboriginal art
found in the United States. While it is more than probable they
were the conception and production of the Indians, they may have
been made by white men and of recent date anterior to their
discovery by Father Marquette, who first saw them about the
first of August, 1673. Marquette was the first white man to des-
cribe the majestic Upper Mississippi, and has therefore been
accredited with its discovery, yet we are satisfied that it had
been not only seen but traversed by other white men nearly
forty years before his discovery. This fact is clearly established
by the Jesuit records. The Franciscan friar, Le Caron, reached
the rivers of Lake Huron in 1616. The Duke de Richelieu obtained a charter, known as the grant of New France, from Louis
XIII, in 1627, which embraced the whole basin of the St. Lawrence and of such streams as flow directly into the sea, also to
the country now known as Florida, and entered upon his possession in 1632, and in 1634 Peres, Brebeuf and Daniel, who were
soon followed by Lallemaid, penetrated the heart of the Huron
wilderness and established two missions and built the first
house of the society of Jesus, and named it St. Ignatius. M.
Nicollet, a French trader, located on the Ottawa river in 1618,
and in 1620 on the border of Lake Huron. Pere Le Jeuni writes
that Nicollet discovered the Wisconsin river in 1639. He says:
"M. Nicollet, who has penetrated farthest into those most dis-
tant regions, has assured me that if he had pushed on three
days longer on a great river which issues from the second lake
of the Hurons (Lake Michigan) he would have found the sea.
Now I strongly suspect this sea is on the north of Mexico, and
that thereby we could have an entrance in Japan and China."
Parkman says: "As early as 1639 Nicollet ascended the Green
Bay of Michigan and crossed the waters of the Mississippi."
While it is improbable that Nicollet saw the Mississippi on his

first visit to Wisconsin in 1634, where he met in one general assembly "four thousand warriors who feasted on six score of beavers before whom he appeared in a robe of state adorned with figures of flowers and birds, approaching with a pistol in each hand he fired both at once, and the astonished natives hence styled him 'Thunder Panther,'" it is more than probable he both found and traversed it in 1639. Father Jean Dequerre went from Sault St. Marie to the Illinois river in 1652 and established a flourishing mission, probably near Starved Rock, possibly at Peoria, Ill. He visited many Indian tribes down that river, and fell a martyr to his faith in the midst of his Christian labors. In 1654 a couple of French fur traders or voyageurs joined a band of Ottawa Indians on an extended hunting expedition to the western wilds, of five hundred leagues, which extended through two years, when they returned accompanied by fifty canoes and two hundred and fifty men. That they not only traversed the "Father of Waters," but followed it from the mouth of the Wisconsin to the mouth of the Mississippi, or even to the gulf, is very probable, but they wrote no history of their trip, as they were upon a hunting, not an exploring voyage. Father Jean Charles Drocoux went from Quebec to the Illinois river and returned in 1657. Pere Renne Mesnard left Quebec on a mission to the far west in 1660, and traversed Lake Superior and thence to Green Bay, reaching Keweena, where he wandered into the forest the next year and was either killed or starved to death. •Father Claude Allouez started on a mission to the far west in 1665, and reached the falls of St. Mary in September, and from thence went to the great village of the Chippewas at Chegoimegon, where a grand intertribal council was held at which the Pottawattamies from Lake Michigan, the Sauks and Foxes from the west, the Hurons from north of Lake Superior, the Sioux from the head waters of the Mississippi, as well as the Illinois, assembled. From these Indians he received a most bewitching description of a noble river flowing south, on which they dwelt, and whose adjacent prairies they assured him were replete with immense herds of buffalo and deer. Their representations created a strong desire in him to explore this Indian paradise. He returned to Quebec in 1667. In 1668 Claude Dablon and Pere Marquette established the mission of St. Marie, which is the oldest European settlement in Michigan. M. Talon, the Canadian intendant, sent Nicholas Perrot on a mission in 1669 to arrange a general conference with all the Indian nations of that locality to assemble at St. Mary. He visited Green Bay, from whence he was escorted by the Pottawattamies to Chicago. In 1669 Allouez visited Green Bay and thence up Fox River of Wisconsin to the principal villages of the Mascoutins, and in the fall of 1670 Dablon joined him when they returned to Green Bay to establish the Mission of St. Xavier. A great congress of the Indian nations was held at St. Mary in May, 1671, where the cross was raised, and by its side a column was planted and marked with the lilies of the Bourbons. The cross was borne by Allouez and Dablon through the lands of the Mascoutins, Kickapoos, Miamis, Sauks and Foxes in Wisconsin and Illinois, so when Father Marquette and Sieur Joliet explored the Fox and the Wisconsin rivers, reaching a Mascoutin village on the bank of the Wisconsin about the 5th of June, 1673, they found the cross erected by Allouez and Dablon in May, 1671, and reaching the Mississippi on the 17th of June, 1673, they descended that great waterway to the mouth of the Missouri. Passing an Indian village about a hundred miles below the mouth of the Wisconsin, they were hospitably received by a band of the Illinois Indians, who welcomed them in the figurative language of the Indian: "Frenchmen, how bright the sun shines when you come to visit us; all our village awaits you, and you shall enter our wigwams in peace." After entering and smoking the calumet they were invited to visit the great chief of the Illinois, and were told by him that the "presence of his guests added flavor to his tobacco, made the river more calm, the sky more serene and the earth more beautiful." Thus it is shown that Nicollet had found and partially, at least, explored the Mississippi thirty-four years before Marquette, and the French fur traders with their escort

of Ottawas had almost to a certainty explored that mighty
river some nineteen years before Marquette and Joliet, so that
it is barely possible that either these traders or Nicollet may
have engraved these monsters upon the rocks for a purpose, but
what that purpose may have been can only be surmised at this
late day. Knowing the superstitious nature of the Indians
these French traders, or voyageurs as they were then called, may
have made their homes in one of the caverns in the cliffs and cut
and delineated those petroglyphs upon the sandstone rock
with the points of their knives for the purpose of frightening
the Indians away from their cavern rendezvous, and thereby
protecting their lives and property, but it is very improbable
that these French voyageurs painted them, for they could hardly
have had the means of doing so, and if they did the storms of
some nineteen years between the time they must have done the
work and the time when Marquette saw them would have
thoroughly obliterated the paint. Another reason why they
did not make those petroglyphs is that they would have fright-
ened their allies—the Ottawas who accompanied them—added
to the fact that white men were seldom known to make petroglyphs, while such works are common to the Indian races, con-
vinces us that they were the entire work of the Indians.

While not disputing the statement of Prof. Russell, herein-
after given, relative to the innumerable human bones he found
in one of these caves, nor attacking his suppositious theory of
their being the work of the Piasa, we suggest that this cave may
have been used as a burial place by the Mound Builders or Indians, where their dead were deposited from generation to generation. It being dry and protected from rains, storms and
dampness, the bones were long in crumbling to decay.

It is a great loss to science and ethnology that the intrusive
changes of the swiftly flowing waters of the Mississippi, together with the rains and storms of two centuries have entirely
obliterated these caves and carried away their deposits, so that
no vestige of them now remains. Nor, indeed, have we any
photographs or other pictures of these monsters *known to be*

accurate. They were delineated on the river side of the rock and destroyed before any efforts were made to even take "counterfeit presentments of them." Hence we only have representations taken from a couple of paintings made from descriptions given by those who were familiar with them. The engravings we herewith give were taken from photographs of these paintings. The one with the elk's horns and serpent's tail was painted by T. F. Ladd, of Whitehall, Ill., the other by an artist sent thither from Washington, D. C., for that purpose. Whether the petroglyphs were made just alike, and the difference between them occurred from painting, or whether they were dissimilar, as shown in the engravings, we cannot say, but presume our engravings are accurate representations of each, and that they were dissimilar as they were delineated on the rock. These petroglyphs were badly marred and defaced before any white man settled in that locality, and though nearly alike in conception and execution they are somewhat dissimilar in the shape of their horns and tail, and the manner of its carriage. The one with the tail passing over the back between the wings, thence over the head and back between the legs, with the fish terminal, comes more closely to Marquette's description than the other, yet in their main features and combination they approximate very closely; and while there were several traditions among the Indians of the then northwest relative to them none but that of the Miamis mention but one monster. Some of the traditions say the Piasa was fond of bathing in the Mississippi and a very rapid swimmer, and when disporting in the tide raised such a commotion in the water as to force great waves over the banks, inundating the adjacent country. Others, that when mad (and it always was mad at the sight of an Indian) it thrashed the ground with its tail until the whole earth shook and trembled. There were several other petroglyphs upon the same strata between Alton and Grafton, but insignificant in size as compared with these. One represented two birds in attitude of fighting over an apple or ring which was carved on the rock between them. Another of a bird and a small animal contending for a similar prize. Another was a small Grecian cross. But we will not attempt to theorize upon these smaller petroglyphs, but refer the reader to the work of the Honorable William McAdams, the ethnologist and archæologist of Alton, Illinois, who either now has or soon will publish a work on the pictographs of the Mississippi Valley, and is of the opinion that these monster petroglyphs, together with the numerous lesser ones of that locality, were a chronological history of the great events which transpired away back in the dim misty past, to some far more intelligent people than the Indian, and is inclined to the belief that they were made by that mysterious but very intelligent pre-historic race of this country, whom we call the Mound Builders, who are only known by the relics of their wonderful works, and what appears from these works to have been their great advancement in a knowledge of the arts and sciences, more especially engineering and fort-building. They also had not only a knowledge of the utility of metal but were experts in the manufacture of copper instruments and hardening them so as to cut granite. They also well understood the art of making pottery and bricks, and must have been as numerous along the banks of the Mississippi as the inhabitants on the banks of the Tiber. While these people might have made these petroglyphs we are clearly of the opinion that they did not, and are the more confirmed in this belief by the fact that they have never heretofore been accredited with keeping any such records, while it is a well settled fact that the Indians not only made petroglyphic records before the advent of the Europeans to this continent but have kept it up ever since. Besides this it is absolutely certain that these petroglyphs were of a more recent date than the age of the Mound Builders, because the elements would have entirely effaced them if not renewed from time to time, which could hardly have been done, since the Mound Builders became extinct thousands of years ago, unless we assume that the Indian is either the descendant of, or the immediate successor to, the possession of this vast continent, neither of which is tenable nor reasonable. The difference in the anatomical formation of these two races forbids this assumption. While the fact that the Indians had no tradition or other evidence of their having overcome and subdued the occupants of this vast country, nor that there were any former people here, establishes beyond doubt that the Indians were in no way connected with the Mound Builders or had any knowledge of their existence, but they utilized their tumuli or mounds for their burial grounds, whereby the name "Indian Mounds" obtains, and even at this late period, when science and research are illuming the dark caverns and hidden nooks of nature's laboratory, there are very many intelligent people who believe these mounds were the production of the Indians. But whether these monster petroglyphs were the conception and work of the red or white man the naked fact still exists that they embodied in a strikingly graphic view so many elements of horror, dread and affright to the Indians of that locality that even the boldest and bravest of them dare not gaze upon the great red eyes and horrid shape of these cold, inanimate pictures, away up on the smooth stone wall, nearly a hundred feet above the river. Such was their dread of them that in passing up and down the Mississippi—which was their only highway at this point—they steered their canoes so as to hug the opposite shore, while few, indeed, dared even look in the direction of the rock whereon these dreaded monsters were delineated, with elevated wings, as if about to swoop down and destroy every living creature upon the broad face of the river. Their position upon the rock was in a straight horizontal line, close together, with their heads facing the east. When discovered by Marquette they seemed to have been recently painted in red, black and green, and were certainly horrid enough in their aspect to frighten the learned and trusting Jesuit, who says, "they frighted me" If they were objects of affright to him how much more so must they have been to the superstitious sons of the forest, who believed in the existence of a multiplicity of real, corporeal, bad spirits, henos, or devils, chief of which was represented by the Piasa—their devil of devils.

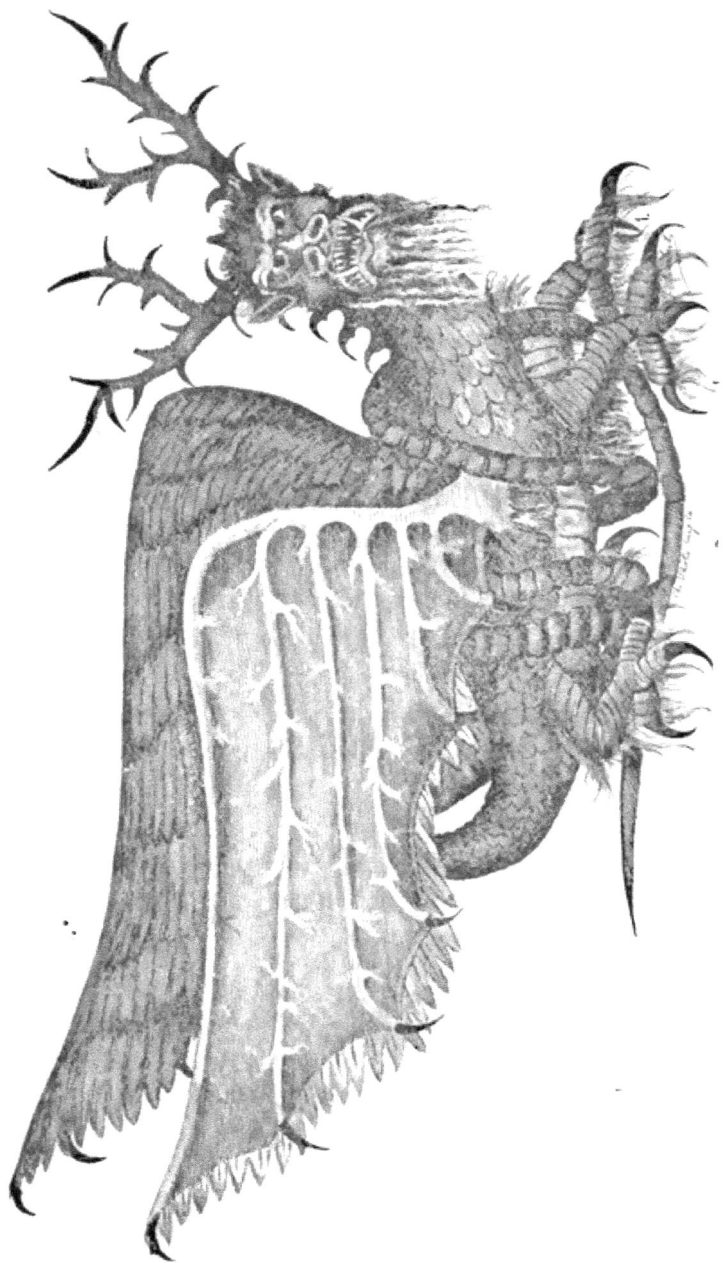

CHAPTER II.

The North American Indians, like the pale faces, have their
historians, orators and statesmen, with this difference in their
production and growth: theirs are carefully selected and edu-
cated to the special profession and make it their life-study and
calling, while ours spring up like magic with a kind of sponta-
neity not unlike Jonah's gourd or mushrooms—the growth of
a single night. Though the Indian has no books and is ignorant of the alphabet and penmanship he has two modes of preserving and recording history — tradition and pictographs or
petroglyphs. The art of preserving history in detail among
the Indians is by tradition, hence its accuracy largely depends
upon the tenacity of the memory of their historians, and the
accuracy with which their traditions are handed down from
father to son, from generation to generation. Their great
events and periods are graphically shown and preserved in
pictographs and petroglyphs as before shown. But they have
no other means of preserving their history in narrative form
and detailed order than tradition.

Though visionary and unreal, still their traditions have much
foundation of fact, and are full of interest to the student and
thinker. The Illini tradition of the Piasa is from the pen of the
late Prof. John Russell, of Jersey county, Illinois, a scholar,

writer and poet of considerable repute. Indeed, his beautiful-
epic entitled, "The Worm of the Still," gave him a world-wide
fame as a poet. He came from the Empire State away back in
the "thirties" and located in Jersey county, where he engaged
in teaching school and writing for the public press. Having
come in almost daily contact with the Indians of that locality,
which is near Alton, where the pictures of these monsters were
delineated, he heard several Indian traditions pertaining to the
Piasa, and was especially interested in that of the Illini or Illinois confederacy, and to fully understand the locality he visited
it in company with a competent guide in March, 1848, and explored the cave near where these monsters were delineated on
the rock, and wrote up the results of his exploration and had
it published in "The Evangelical Magazine and Gospel Advo-
cate," printed and published at Utica, in the State of New York,
in the July number, 1848, and republished in the February
number of "Manford's Magazine," of Chicago, 1887, which is
as follows:

"THE PIASA; AN INDIAN TRADITION OF ILLINOIS.

"No part of the United States, not even the highlands of the
Hudson, can vie in wild and romantic scenery with the bluffs of
Illinois. On one side of the river, often at the water's edge, a
perpendicular wall of rock rises to the height of some hundred
feet. Generally on the opposite shore is a level bottom or prai-
rie of several miles in width, extending to a similar bluff that
runs parallel with the river. One of these ranges commences at
Alton and extends, with a few intervals, for many miles along
the left bank of the Illinois. In descending the river to Alton
the traveler will observe between that town and the mouth of
the Illinois a narrow ravine, through which a small stream dis-
charges its waters into the Mississippi. The stream is the
Piasa. Its name is Indian, and signifies in the Illini, "the bird
that devours men." Near the mouth of that stream, on the
smooth and perpendicular face of the bluff, at an elevation
which no human art can reach, is cut the figure of an enormous

bird, with its wings extended. The bird which this figure represents was called by these Indians the Piasa, and from this is derived the name of the stream. The tradition of the Piasa is still current among all the tribes of the Upper Mississippi, and those who have inhabited the valley of the Illinois, and is briefly this: 'Many thousand moons before the arrival of the pale-faces, when the great Magalonyx and Mastodon, whose bones are now dug up, were still living in the land of the green prairies, there existed a bird of such dimensions that he could easily carry off in his talons a full grown deer. Having obtained a taste of human flesh from that time he would prey upon nothing else. He was artful as he was powerful, and would dart suddenly and unexpectedly upon an Indian, bear him off into one of the caves of the bluff and devour him. Hundreds of warriors attempted for years to destroy him, but without success. Whole villages were nearly depopulated, and consternation spread through all the tribes of the Illini. At length *Ouatogo, a chief whose fame extended even beyond the great lakes, separating himself from the rest of his tribe, fasted in solitude for the space of the whole moon and prayed to the Great Spirit, the Master of Life, that he would protect his children from the Piasa. On the last night of his fast the Great Spirit appeared to Ouatogo in a dream, and directed him to select twenty of his warriors, each armed with a bow and poisoned arrow, and conceal them in a designated spot. Near the place of their concealment another warrior was to stand in open view as a victim for the Piasa, which they must shoot the instant that he pounced upon his prey. When the chief awoke the next morning he thanked the Great Spirit, and returning to his tribe told them the dream. The warriors were quickly selected and placed in ambush as directed. Ouatogo offered himself as the victim. He was willing to die for his tribe. Placing himself in open view of the bluff he soon saw the Piasa perched on the cliff, eyeing his

---

*WAW-TO'-GO.

prey. Ouatogo drew up his manly form to its utmost height, planting his feet firmly upon the earth he began to chant the death song of an Indian warrior. A moment after the Piasa arose into the air and swift as the thunderbolt darted down upon the chief. Scarcely had he reached his victim when every bow was sprung and every arrow sent to the feather into his body. The Piasa uttered a wild, fearful scream, that resounded far over the opposite side of the river, and expired. Ouatogo was safe. Not an arrow, not even the talons of the bird had touched him. The Master of Life, in admiration of the generous deed of Ouatogo, had held over him an invisible shield. In memory of this event the image of the Piasa was engraven on the face of the bluff.' Such is the Indian tradition. Of course I do not vouch for its truth. This, however, is certain, the figure of a large bird cut in the solid rock is still there, and at a height that is perfectly inaccesable. How and for what purpose it was made I leave for others to determine. Even at this day an Indian never passes that spot in his canoe without firing his gun at the figure of the bird. The marks of the balls are almost innumerable. Near the close of March of the present year I was induced to visit the bluffs below the mouth of the Illinois and above the Piasa. My curiosity was principally directed to the examination of a cave connected with the above tradition, as one of those to which the bird had carried his victims. Preceded by an intelligent guide, who carried a spade, I set out on my excursion. The cave was extremely difficult of access, and at one point of our progress I stood at an elevation of one hundred and fifty feet on the face of the perpendicular bluff, with barely room to sustain one foot. The unbroken wall towered above me, while below was the river. After a long and perilous clambering we reached the cave, which was about fifty feet above the surface of the river By the aid of a long pole, placed on a projecting rock and the upper end touching the mouth of the cave, we succeeded in entering it. The Mississippi was rolling in silent grandeur beneath us; high over our heads a single cedar hung its branches over the cliff, on the blasted top of which was seated a bald eagle. No other sound or sign of life was near us. A Sabbath stillness rested on the scene. Not a cloud was visible in the the heavens, not a breath of air was stirring. The broad Mississippi lay before us calm and smooth as a lake. The landscape presented the same wild aspect as it did before it had met the eyes of the white man. The roof of the cavern was vaulted, the top of which was hardly less than twenty feet high. The shape of the cave was irregular, but so far as I could judge the bottom would average twenty by thirty feet. *The floor of the cave throughout its whole extent was one mass of human bones.* Skulls and other bones were mingled together in the utmost confusion. To what depth they extended I am unable to decide, but we dug to the depth of three or four feet in every quarter of the cavern and still we found only bones. *The remains of thousands must have been deposited there.* How and by whom and for what purpose it is impossible to conjecture."

Such is the tradition of the dread Piasa, as given by Prof. Russell, as common among the great confederation known as the Illini. His statement that the place where this monster was delineated was so high that no human art could reach it shows that he had but little knowledge of the use of blocks and pulleys as a means of reaching elevated places. To the painter of the present day eighty feet elevations have no terror and offer but little inconvenience. We think he made a mistake in saying the wings of this monster were represented as being extended. He probably intended to use the words " elevated, as in the act of starting to fly," which would be more strictly in accordance with the position of the wings, as shown by the engravings, or, in the language of the evangelist, " their wings were stretched upward." It will be observed that each wing has five hook-shaped pendants, representing dagger-shaped horns, which may have been intended to represent the ten horns of the great red dragon described in Revelations. While Pere Marquette called them monsters, Prof. Russell called it (for he only mentioned one) a bird; and indeed, it, or they, may have been called bird, beast, saurian or reptile with equal propriety, since all are combined in the representation, with a little of the man thrown in to make this wonderful combination of aerial, mundane and saurian — *what is it?*

From the fact that the Mississippi is liable to wash out new channels and change its course, the strong probability is that at the time these petroglyphs were made its channel was considerably south of its present one and that there was a large depth of earth lying at the base of the present perpendicular stone wall which extended up to the bed of the sandstone on which they were cut, so that the artist—for he who conceived and executed them was an artist of marked ability—stood upon the ground to do his work, and that since then the swift waters of the "Father of Waters" have cut out its present channel, sweeping the earth into the gulf, leaving these monster petroglyphs some eighty feet above the river's surface. Assuming this to be true their elevation is no wonder. When and by what tribe, nation or confederation of Indians the particular locality about Alton, Ill., was first settled, like the origin of the Indian race, is an unsolved and in all human probability ever will remain an unsolvable mystery, unless we adopt the theory advanced by some ethnologists and beg the question by saying, they are indigenous to the Western Hemisphere, or, like Topsy, were "never born but 'growed.'" Others advance the hypothesis of their being the offspring of that wonderful people of whom we see so much and know so little—the Mound Builders. The advocates of this theory urge as a reason for their belief their divergence from all European nations in their physical structure and color. Prominent among points of difference is the fact that in the pile or hair of the European the coloring matter is distributed by means of a central canal, while in the Indian it is incorporated in the fibrous structure; but the most clearly defined difference is in the shape of the hair under the microscope. That of the Indian being round; the white man,

oval; the negro, flat. If these stolid, lazy, ignorant, hunting
and fishing people are the descendants of the once powerful,
intelligent, industrious, pastoral Mound Builders, then, indeed,
may we exclaim, in the language of Mark Antony, "O, my
countrymen, what a fall was there!" Others claim that they
are a derivative race, and sprang from some of the ancient Asi-
atics, while others assert, with considerable reason to back
them, that they are the offspring of the lost tribes of Israel, described by Esdras, "these are the ten tribes which were carried
away prisoners out of their own land in the time of Osea, the
king, whom Salamanaser, the king of Assyria, led away captive
into another land. But they took this counsel among them-
selves, that they would leave the multitude of the heathen and
go forth into a farther country, where never mankind dwelt.
And they entered into Euphrates by the narrow passage of the
river. For the Most High then showed signs for them and held
still the flood till they were passed over. For through that
country there was a great way to go, namely, of a year and a
half, and the same region is called Asareth." By assuming that
away back in the early days when "the waters were being
divided and gathered together in one place, and the dry land
appeared" the western limits of America were united to Asia
on the west and Europe on the east, we can readily see how the
Indians as well as animals from the present Eastern Hemisphere
crossed over to this. Though, like the ancient Scythians, the Indians scalped their victims and tortured their prisoners; and like the
Tartars, in the shape of their canoes and manner of marching
in single file, the great similarity of their religious customs and
habits to those of the ancient Jews in many of their leading
characteristics, among which were their offering sacrifices and
burnt-offerings to appease and please their deities, and celebra-
ting the passover in their harvest or crane dance, are, indeed,
very strong arguments in favor of their Hebrew origin and
descent. Yet no generally accepted theory or hypothesis has
been accepted by the ethnologists upon this question, so we are

left in the dark to grope our way to the light as best we can. We have given much time and study to the mythologies, customs, habits and religious practices of the Indians, which has confirmed our belief in their Jewish origin, and that they probably came to this continent away back of the Christian era, and are possibly the descendants of the lost tribes of Israel, described by Esdras in the Apocrypha, as before indicated. When the white people first discovered the Upper Mississippi nearly all of its banks and adjacent country were in the full and undisputed possession of a powerful Indian confederacy, known as the Illini. This confederacy was originally composed of possibly fifty Indian nations, united under one set of sachems or chiefs, and originally came from the shores of the Gulf of Mexico and banks of the various streams entering it. Having lived there for centuries they from time to time ascended the Mississippi, each time going a little farther up they finally took complete possession of that great river with its adjacent lands. The powerful and warlike Miamis, according to their tradition, were once a member of that great confederacy, and had their principal village at or near where the city of Alton, Illinois, now stands. Their tradition was related to us nearly sixty years ago by a chief, and is substantially as follows:

THE MIAMI TRADITION OF THE PIASA.

Several thousand winters before the pale-faces came to this country there existed the most powerful Indian confederacy ever known. Their principal country was upon the bank of the broad water, into which the Mestchecepe (now spelled Mississippi), or great river, flows. Here they lived and were prosperous and happy for many thousand winters. Their warriors became as numerous as the trees in the forest, and were as brave as the bear, strong as the buffalo, swift as the elk and cunning as the fox. Their long residence and great multitude in that country resulted in killing off the buffalo, elk, moose and deer, until game became so scarce that their hunters were forced to keep constantly extending their hunting grounds farther north, and the Mestchecepe being their principal highway they ascended

that great river in their canoes, but frequently came in contact
and conflict with other tribes, always overcoming and conquer-
ing them; for it was the pride and glory of the warriors of this
confederacy that they were Illini, which signified in their language, 'we are men, not dogs or cowards.' As their hunting
parties advanced up the Mestchecepe their families followed,
until they reached the great lakes in the north. When they
reached the country about the mouth of the Missouri, or muddy
river, and thence up to the mouth of the Illinois, and up that
stream to its source they found the entire surrounding country
full of game of every kind known to them, in exhaustless quan-
tities. Its woods abounded in fruits, flowers, nuts and wild
honey of the richest flavor and sweetest taste; while its creeks,
rivers and lakes teemed with fish and eel so thick as to impede
their navigation, even by canoe. In short, it was a perfect
Indian paradise.

> "Where corn, tobacco, squash and bean,
> Luxuriant to the view,
> In one unbroken round was seen,
> The gift of Manitou."

Immense herds of buffalo, moose, elk and deer listlessly roam-
ed over the broad savannas, daintily nipping earth's luxuriant
beard—the grass—too fat and happy to even heed the approach
of the Indian hunter.

> "In such a paradise the game
> Of every species, every name,
> Was quickly found on every hand,
> To rich reward the hunter band."

Here the lordly Indian could, with but little effort on his part,
daily feast upon

> Roast bear and bison, elk and moose.
> Roast deer and turkey, brant and goose,
> Baked woodchuck, antelope and coon,
> Baked squirrel, rabbit, duck and loon,
> Broiled pheasant, chicken, lark and quail,
> Broiled woodcock, plover, snipe and rail,
> Fried lobster, turtle, fish and crabs,
> Fried eels and clams, fried eggs and squabs,
> Boiled maize, potatoes, rice and squash,
> Boiled pumpkins, beans and succotash,
> Parched acorns, artichokes and corn,
> Parched roots and nuts of various form,
> Wild apples, cherries, grapes and plum,
> Wild berries and wild honey-comb.

Powerful in numbers, they soon became lax in discipline, because they were so much dreaded by surrounding nations that they were never attacked. Naturally lazy, their easy lives led to indolent habits and reckless living, united to a long period of peaceful relations between them and their surrounding nations drove the cultivation of the art of war into "innoxious desuetude." Their great numerical strength and slothful habits resulted with them as with every other great nation in being the rock upon which their confederacy was broken and shattered to atoms, never again to be united, for it is a fact that the cohesive attraction which holds an Indian nation together is weakened as the nation increases in size. The larger the number the greater the prize in reaching its chief command, which offers temptations to the unscrupulous and ambitious leaders of each powerful gentes or phratry to intrigue and plot for its command, which sooner or later results in a complete rupture, generally ending in a bitter, if not exterminating, internal war. The Illini became insolent, oppressive and greedy to such a degree as to forget the greatest of all Indian virtues—hospitality to strangers—when the Great Spirit determined to punish them as He did the inhabitants of Sodom and Gomorrah, because they had become thoroughly wicked and transgressed His law. First afflicting them with the most dreaded plague to the Indians—small-pox—which carried away thousands upon thousands; and scarcely had this plague subsided ere He sent evil spirits among them to encourage and inaugurate jealousies, intrigues, plots and revolts, not only among the confederacy, but among the different tribes composing it. Assassinations, murders and revolutions followed until the once almost omnipotent Illini were severed and torn to segments by internal wars. Nor did their afflictions end with the collapse of the confederacy, but the most implacable wars sprang up between the broken segments of the Illini, which not infrequently terminated in the utter annihilation of some of its tribes. The Miamis and Mestchegamies (generally spelled Michigamies) were among the most powerful tribes or nations of the Illini, and their territories joined each other, while their principal villages were only some twenty miles apart, both on the north bank of the Meschecepe, one near the mouth of the Illinois, the other near where Alton now stands. A bitter and relentless war had been carried on between these two nations, which had been friends and allies for generations before. Murders and robberies were of such daily occurrence that hunting and fishing parties were compelled to go in large bodies, ever ready to repel attacks. Each nation had a lookout or signal station, where sentinels were always on duty to signal everything which might indicate approaching danger. That of the Mestchegamies was upon the upper, the Miamis the lower, point of the rock promontory, extending almost continuously between their villages. Overlying the rocks there was sufficient soil to support the growth of large oak trees, on the limbs of which platforms of poles were made for their sentinels. Each sentry-tree commanded a view of the surface of the Mestchecepe between the two villages and over the bluff on the south; but owing to several deep ravines leading from the north, cutting their path through the promontory to reach the river, an army might pass along some of these canyons or ravines without being seen from either of their lookouts. There were two caves entering the rock near the lower end of the promontory, some fifty feet above the river's current, in which two huge monsters, with the body and claws of an alligator, wings of an eagle, but ten times larger; horns of an elk or deer, ears of a fox, face of a man, mouth, teeth and beard of a tiger, and tail of a serpent or fish, made their homes, but spent the greater part of their time resting and dozing upon some high part of the rocks, or flying over the country. One of these was fond of bathing, and a good swimmer; while the other seemed to be delighted with its ability to beat the earth with its monstrous bony tail. Though of horrid shape and mien they had never molested the Indians other than by their loud noises. The voice of one resembled the roaring of a buffalo bull, the other the shrill scream of the panther. They had lived there so long without doing violence to the Miamis that they considered them good spirits, and were very careful about disturbing or scaring them away, notwithstanding the Indians knew these monsters as devil-birds, and that they were of sufficient strength to pick up and carry off a young buffalo, and in fact lived and battened on deer, elk and young buffalo, upon which they swooped down and clutched with their powerful claws or talons and bore off to their cavern homes in the cliff to devour at their leisure.

Thus matters stood until one bright September morn, when the Mestchegamies left their village in force to steal a march upon and stealthily attack their mortal foes; and on that same morning the Miamis attempted to play the same game upon the Mestchegamies. The latter got the earlier start and reached the upper end of the lower Piasa canyon as the Miamis reached its lower end. Each were intending a surprise and slaughter of their enemies by passing through this canyon, the Miamis up, the Mestchegamies down it. Both sides were in force and fully armed for war. Soon they came face to face in the narrow canyon, where escape from a desperate battle was impossible except by abject flight. But no such thought was entertained by either side. With the war-whoop of their respective nations the dread battle shock was inaugurated. Every brave and warrior resolved to conquer or die in the narrow defile. Quarter was neither given nor expected. In the midst of this fierce and bloody encounter, and at a moment when the ranks of the Mestchegamies were wavering as if about to yield or fly, two dread monsters, like the war horse of the Scriptures "snift the battle from afar" and came flying up the canyon, uttering bellowings and shrieks, while the flapping of their wings upon the air roared out like so many thunderclaps. Passing close over the heads of the combatants each selected and picked up in his huge talons a Miami chieftain and bore him off above the now terrified and utterly demoralized Miamis, who believed the Great Spirit had sent these dread monsters, or bad spirits, to aid and assist their enemies. And as each bore away in its cruel claws a struggling, squirming, howling, groaning, screaming chieftain, the horrified Miamis, distinctly heard them calling, pleading and imploring for assistance, which they could not give; the bravest heart ceased to beat and the strongest limbs were paralyzed with terror. They were incapable of either thought or act until aroused to a sense of their position by the fierce war-whoop of the Mestehegamies, who were now sure of victory, since the Great Spirit had sent these monsters to fight their battles for them. All order was gone from the Miamis, and their leaders being carried away by the monsters, a panic set in and ran riot through the ranks, and thousands were slaughtered by the fierce Mestehegamies or forced into the Mississippi by the terrible onslaught and drowned. Instead of a battle it was a massacre—a holocaust, which only ceased with the close of day, since the Indians never fight in the darkness of the night. Though by no means annihilated the Miamis were so badly crippled as a nation that they fled towards the Wabash and crossed that stream ere they felt safe. Here they remained during generation after generation,

> "Gathering their brows like gathering storm
> Nursing their wrath to keep it warm,"

never forgetting nor forgiving the Mestehegamies or the monsters, but like Hamilcar, the Carthagenian, who caused his son, Hannibal, to swear eternal enmity to Rome, each father related it to his son from generation to generation, and swore them to avenge the terrible massacre of their ancestors in the canyon on the Mestcheeepe.

In the meanwhile the Mestehegamies had reunited with the Peorias, Cohokias, Tamaroas and Kaskaskias, forming another confederacy known as the Illinois. Though less formidable in numerical strength than their predecessors the Illini, the Illinois were a very powerful and warlike confederacy, and soon became the absolute owners and masters of a vast territory, bounded on the east by the Wabash, south and west by the

Metschecepe, running north almost to Lake Michigan. They soon became a proud, haughty, domineering and extremely selfish confederacy, and guarded their rights of territory with rigorous exactitude. Every trespass upon their hunting grounds was promptly and severely punished. The closer they guarded their territory against trespass from the hunters of surrounding tribes the greater was their temptation; for the Indian like Mother Eve, has a strong desire for forbidden fruit, and feels bound to do that which he is forbidden to do if it breaks his neck. Hence large hunting parties were formed and raids made into the territory of the Illinois, which exasperated them in turn, resulting in numerous murders and small battles, followed by a few cold-blooded massacres. In this way the passions of these naturally vengeful people were wrought up to a white heat, when nothing but revenge and slaughter was thought of. This was the long-wished and patiently waited for time for the Miamis to wipe out the score between them and the Mestchegamies, for

" Time at last sets all things even,
And if we do but watch the hour,
There never yet was human power
Which could evade, if unforgiven,
The patient search and vigil long,
Of him who treasures up a wrong."

Generation after generation had come and gone to find the Miamis plotting, planning and scheming some means of paying off their deadly enemies the full amount of their sufferings and loss, not only in their own coin, but with compound interest. By persistent and untiring efforts they succeeded in organizing a powerful Indian confederacy, about the year 1760, known as the Peuotomies, which was composed of many, if not quite all the Indian nations of the then northwest who spoke the Algonkian language; among whom the Miamis, Pottawattamies, Ottawas, Chippewas, Sauks and Foxes were prominent actors in the long and sanguinary struggle which followed close upon the formation of the Peuotomies. Revenge has ever been the controlling passion of the Indian, impelling him to fight like a demon for its accomplishment. This was the strongest incentive to the Penotomies in the war, to which was added a desire for the possession of the magnificent territory of the Illinois. The great war chief, Sugar, of the Pottawattamies, was their commander-in-chief. His height, as shown by a measurement of his skeleton made by us in 1831, must have been six feet six inches; while his weight certainly approached three hundred pounds. (He was buried in a wooden pen on the south bank of the Illinois river, a few miles above Starved Rock.) Big Elk, the war chief the Mestehegamies, commanded the Illinois, who were not only fighting for revenge upon their enemies on account of numerous murders and robberies committed on them by the Penotomies, but for everything dear to the Indian—home, country, and the graves of their sires.

With such prizes to contend for, and such armies to contend, the war was not only terrific but long and implacable. Commencing near the Wabash above Vincennes in the early spring it lasted until the following winter. Step by step the Penotomies drove the Illinois from point to point, fighting as they went, until they reached Blue Island, near Chicago, where a most terrific battle took place, lasting several days, which resulted in, not only the defeat of the Illinois, but in breaking up their army and scattering them in segments and ignominious flight. A considerable portion of them however, under Big Elk, fled down the Des Plaines river to the place where the city of Joliet now stands, where they were overtaken by the Penotomies, flushed with their late signal victory. Here another sanguinary battle occurred, in which the Illinois fought with desperation, but were again defeated with great slaughter. From here they again fled down the Illinois river, but were overtaken at the point where the city of Morris now stands, where another severe struggle ensued, resulting in a victory for the Penotomies, but at the cost of the lives of many of their bravest and best soldiers, among whom was the great Chippewa chief—Nucquette—who was buried in one of the tumuli near where he fell, and a red cedar pole placed at the head of his grave to mark the spot. **This** pole still stands where it was put over a hundred and twenty-five years ago, and is now in a good state of preservation, and is located on Wauponsee street, near the Court House, in Morris. The loss of the Illinois in this battle was far greater than that of their enemies, and again they fled down the Illinois, endeavoring to descend that river to the Mississippi, but were overtaken by the victorious Peuotomies, who not only cut off their passage down that river but surrounded them on all sides, thus cutting off every avenue of escape. Standing on the south bank of the Illinois river, about eight miles below the city of Ottawa, **is** a singularly shaped St. Peter's sandstone rock, which rises up from the river's edge one hundred and forty-seven feet. Its surface embraces an area of about half an acre, and is overlaid with earth several feet deep, studded with a few small red cedar **trees.** It is circular in shape and its walls are nearly perpendicular, **except a small space on** the south side, where persons **can climb up.** But this passage way is so narrow that it was easily defended by those on its summit. In their sore need and desperate extremity, the remnant of the Illinois, who had fled in this direction with Big Elk, their chief, sought refuge upon this rock. But the beseigers at once surrounded the rock, holding their lines beyond the reach of the arrows of the beseiged; and thus cut off all supplies of food. There were crevices worn in the face of this rock immediately above the water in the river, so deep and large as to permit an Indian to pass all along the river side of the rock, so when the famishing beseiged lowered **a vessel by** means of a rawhide string for water an Indian in the crevice below seized the string and jerked the drawer head foremost from the rock into the river, a distance of nearly one hundred and fifty feet. To avoid this certain death the water-drawers ran their leather cords around the body of a tree or stump, unwinding it slowly, and thus lowered their water vessels down. But this proved abortive, for the Peuotomies, who were stationed along the crevices below, cut the cord with their scalping knives, and, being sheltered by the projecting rock above they could not be dislodged by the Illinois. Thus were the besieged completely cut off from food and water, without which they could live but a few days at best. The segment of the Illinois here penned up on this cold inhospitable rock were chiefly Mestchegamies, the mortal foes of the Miamis, while the latter were their most insatiable tormentors, and ever and anon kept shouting to them: "Now send forth your devil-birds for food and water; call forth your Piasas to keep you from the Panguk (god of death), whose chattering teeth are tearing and rending your trembling cowardly bodies." To these cruel taunts the brave but now famishing Mestchegamies hurled back their defiance: "The Miamis are dogs and squaw-pappooses, who fight only with their mouths and dare not meet men face to face in fair battle. If you will allow us to come down from this rock and meet us on the plain, weak and hungry as we are, we will send you flying like so many howling coyotes, as our ancestors did in the canyon on the Mestchecepe long ago, and that, too, without assistance from devil-birds or Piasas." Nor were thirst and famine the only enemies the Illinois were forced to contend with; winter, stern, cold and stormy, had set in. The angry winds howled over and around this perpendicular rock like searching demons, from whose piercing shafts they had no shelter, nor were they half clad. This small high rock is but a dissevered part of the south bluff of the Illinois river, and its height is no greater than the next point of the rock bluff immediately east, and is separated from it by a deep gulch, about two hundred yards wide at the top. Upon this last named point the Chevalier La Salle erected a Fort, surrounded with ditches and embankments, in November, 1682, and called it Fort St. Louis, in honor of the then King of France. Fort St. Louis was occupied and held by Tonti, the one armed Italian lieutenant under La Salle until 1702 or a period of twenty years; but no vestige, save the ditches and earthen breast-

works, remained at the seige of the Illinois on Starved
Rock. Many of the Peuotomies, more especially the Miamis
and Pottawattamies, were armed with rifles or muskets, and
experts in their use; and by lying down behind the earthen
embankments of the old fort they could pick off the Illinois on
Starved Rock, which was within easy rifle range. Thus instead
of a refuge and place of safety, Starved Rock proved to be a
death trap and a snare to the Illinois. What between thirst,
hunger, cold and the deadly bullets of their implacable enemies
their tortures were worse than those described in Dante's In-
ferno. Bearing all like heroes as they were, the physically fee-
ble Illinois made a dash for life and liberty the first dark night
after their entrapment by climbing down from the rock and
rushing through the beleaguering lines. Eleven only of their entire number succeeded in making good their escape. All the
rest who were able to leave the rock that cold, stormy night,
crossed the dark and silent trail from which there is no return.
Thus perished this remnant of the Illinois who sought safety
on this rock, which from thence forward has been known by
no other name than *Starved Rock*.

Though badly defeated in this long and bloody war the Illinois were by no means crushed out of existence, but the Mestchegamies were virtually annihilated, never again to be
known among the red men save by tradition. Thus at
last were the Miamis terribly avenged upon their bitterest
enemies after waiting and watching for an opportunity generation after generation. As the result of this long war the Illinois
were confined to the territory in southern Illinois, and the Miamis regained their ancient village and territory surrounding
Alton, Illinois. But upon their return, after an absence of a
thousand moons, they found the image of the devil-bird or
Piasa upon the rock near where these monsters had been the
cause of their great loss of life and conntry, which fact had been
kept green in their minds by tradition, and could they have
reached the place of their delineation upon the perpendicular

wall they doubtless would have effaced them so that no mark or even scratch should indicate where they were. But as the place was some eighty feet high they were compelled to wreak their spite and hate upon these cold images by shooting at and cursing them. If these traditions are true, then, indeed, the temporary assistance of the Piasa to the Mestehegamics in their desperate battle with the Miamis, in the canyon near Alton, Illinois, instead of a blessing proved to be a terrible curse to them, soon after, by the great sacrifice of their people to feed the ever hungry monsters which seemed to have a special taste for Indian flesh, and would touch no other. The time when the Piasa existed in this country, according to the Illini tradition, was "many thousand moons before the arrival of the pale-faces," while that of the Miamis says, "several thousand winters before the pale-faces came." Though indefinite as to the exact time or period both indicate a very long period of time—many centuries—and may be construed to go away back to the mesozoic or middle-life geological period, known as the age of reptiles, when the monster saurians existed in great numbers and varieties, among which were the ichthyosaur, with the general shape of the dolphin, snout of the porpoise, head of the lizard, jaws and teeth of the crocodile, vertebra of the fish, sternal arch of the water-mole, paddles of the whale, trunk and tail of a quadruped. It had a short, thick neck, large head, enormous mouth, with as high as 160 long, round, sharp teeth. It had for its playmate and companion another monster called the plesiosaur, with the head of a lizard, feet of a crocodile, neck of a swan, trunk and tail of a quadruped, ribs of the chameleon and paddles of the whale. His body was shorter and much larger than that of his companion, while in general size they were nearly equal. And there were other monsters in those days, among the most notable of which were the pterodactyl, or wing-finger-ed monstrosity, which in every point of the horrible surpassed the ichthyosaur and plesiosaur. It was an aerial beast, bird or reptile, with wings shaped like those of the bat. Its bones were hollow like those of the bird, but it had no feathers, and though its bill resembled that of the bittern, it was full of long, sharp teeth like those of the shark. Instead of two legs and feet it had four of each. The fore legs seemed to have come out at the butt of its wings and rested upon them. In shape they resembled human arms, with talons like the eagle in shape but much longer. It probably could walk on its hind legs with folded wings. Its legs, like its arms, were supplied with long and powerful talons. Its spread of wings was from fifteen to twenty-five feet. The fossil remains of some twenty-five species of this monster have been found, and it is sometimes called the ptero-saur or flying lizzard. There were other monster lizards in those days, some of which were nearly or quite one hundred feet long, known as dinosaurs (terrible lizzards), megalosaurs, hylaeosaurs, iguanadons, etc. The megalosaur, as shown by the skeleton restored and now in the Crystal Palace at Sy-denham, England, is really a most hideous monster, with im-mense body, legs and tail, all covered with armor scales. Another great monster of the frog species, called the labyrinth-odon, then lived. Its general shape was that of a frog, but it had the teeth of an alligator, while its head was protected by a natural helmet and its body with scales. But the most singular monster of the age yet discovered and its shape and component parts analyzed is the ramphorhyncus, which seems to be a con-nective link between birds, beasts and reptiles. Its body and neck resemble that of the Piasa, while its tail is identical with it, except it is pictured as dragging behind instead of being carried around the body or over its back and head. The shape of the head is drawn to resemble that of a duck, with the long bill of a snipe or bittern, but is full of sharp, round teeth, like those of the crocodile It had four legs, with eagle's talons, and a pair of bat-like wings. When on the ground it traveled on all fours, dragging its long tail trailing behind, and when flying it must have wrapped it around its body, under its wings or around its huge neck. Its entire length from head to tip of tail was probably thirty feet or more. In many respects the Piasa is a faithful copy of the ramphorhyncus. The form, shape and description of the Piasa, according to the Indian traditions were painted from actual sight of the living subject; that of the ramphorhyncus is from collecting its badly decomposed bones, and from their form, shape and size constructing an ideal monster.

We are strongly of the opinion that they were but one and the same species, and that the Indians' representation upon the rock is by far the truer one of this extinct monster. While there are several close resemblances between the pterodactyl and the Piasa, as shown in the petroglyphs, the similarity between them and the ramphorhyncus is more strikingly clear. Thus may the traditions of these Indians be true, and their petroglyphic history of the Piasa may enable the scientist to reconstruct his ramphorhyncus into the shape and form of the Indians' Piasa. If these petroglyphs were the work of the Indian, and of this we have but little doubt, they show that he had a knowledge, real or traditional, of the existence of these monsters of the geological reptile age. And it is true that many of the finest specimens of these extinct monsters, as well as those of the post-tertiary period, have been found in the United States. The bad lands of Arizona and the cretaceous rocks of the State of Kansas are specially prolific in the production of skeletons of the extinct saurians*, while the bones of the mastodon and other monsters of the tertiary period are scattered all over this country. Our conclusions may be summed up in a few words, as follows:

First. The Indians appeared upon this continent before the extinction of the huge reptiles and saurians of the mesozoic age.

Second. That among the still existing saurians or reptiles when the Indians appeared was one huge monster that could walk, run, fly and swim, known to the Indians as the Piasa whose bones have been found and reconstructed into the saurian, or reptile, known to science as the ramphorhyncus.

---

*The best specimens of the anatomy of the ramphorhyncus ever found was lately discovered by Prof. Marsh in Kansas.

Third. That **this saurian** or reptile **was of immense** size, great strength and voracious appetite with decidedly cannibal propensities, and feasted **upon** Indian **flesh.**

Fourth. **That these petroglyphs** were made by the **Indians** many centuries after the extinction of these **monsters as a** means of preserving and refreshing their tradition; or, in other words, their tradition **was a** very old one while these petroglyphs were comparatively of recent date and made by persons who never saw the **Piasa,** but made them to correspond with **the descriptions given in their** tradition.

And lastly the manifest similarity and close analogy between the noble, patriotic and heroic conduct of this great Indian chief, Ouatogo, in offering himself as the victim of the dread Piasa to save his nation from utter destruction and annihilation upon the banks of the majestic Mississippi to that of the Chief of all Chieftains, Immanuel, in offering up his young life upon the cross on Mount Calvary, as a sacrifice and propitiation for the sins of **the** world, **is** such as to attract our special wonder, while the simple but beautiful faith of these **sons of** the forest in the loving kindness and **ever watchful care of an all-over-ruling power,** **as expressed in the few words,** "the Great Spirit held an invis**ible** shield over Ouatogo which protected him from the talons **of the monster, and the arrows of his men,"** challenges our ad**miration. Thus in the character of** Ouatogo do we see a type and symbol **of "the Lamb of God that** taketh away the sin of **the world."**

www.ingramcontent.com/pod-product-compliance
Lightning Source LLC
Chambersburg PA
CBHW032122080426
42733CB00008B/1022